EGGHEAD

EGGHEAD

or, You Can't Survive on Ideas Alone

BO BURNHAM

drawings by CHANCE BONE

GRAND CENTRAL
PUBLISHING

NEW YORK   BOSTON

The characters and events in this book are fictitious. Any similarity to real persons, living or dead, is coincidental and not intended by the author.

Grand Central Publishing
Hachette Book Group
1290 Avenue of the Americas
New York, NY 10104

www.HachetteBookGroup.com

Printed in the United States of America

LSC-C

Originally published in hardcover by Hachette Book Group.

First trade edition: October 2014

10 9

Grand Central Publishing is a division of Hachette Book Group, Inc.
The Grand Central Publishing name and logo are trademarks of Hachette Book Group, Inc.

The Hachette Speakers Bureau provides a wide range of authors for speaking events. To find out more, go to www.hachettespeakersbureau.com or call (866) 376-6591.

The publisher is not responsible for websites (or their content) that are not owned by the publisher.

Library of Congress Control Number: 2013941570

ISBN 978-1-4555-1913-2 (pbk.)

For you, hopefully.

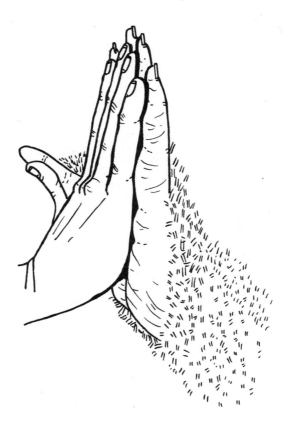

Effortless

Writing poetry is effortless,
heifer piss, lever kiss,
Trevor, Chris...
...whoops, got a little light-headed.

A Dog's Poem

Roses are grey,
violets are a different shade of grey,
let's go chase cars!

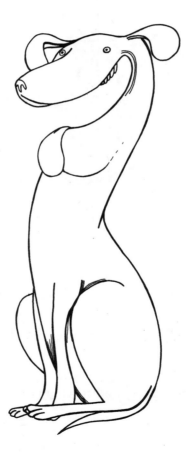

Kiss You

I want to kiss you all day.
I want to start at dawn.
I want our mouths to dry out by breakfast.
I want our jaws to start cramping by noon.
I want us to question our decision to kiss all day by
  hour five.
I want to have sex really quickly then seriously stop
  all this kissing bullshit because you need your
  personal space, apparently.

The Squares

The Squares lived happily,
in their square houses,
in their square yards,
in their square town.

One day, a family of Circles
moved in from the west.

"Get out of here, roundies!" shouted one of the Squares.
"Why?" asked one of the Circles.
"Because this is a metaphor for racism!"

Convenience

I would do anything for you,
if convenient.

I would move a mountain for you
if that mountain could be moved
with a button or with a lever that
wasn't too cold to the touch.

I would give you the moon if I could.
You would love the moon. You would
show it off to everyone and not give a fuck
that you've now severely damaged our ecosystem
    by disrupting the tides.

Maybe a nice look in the mirror is in order, Missy.

Magic

Read this to yourself. Read it silently.
Don't move your lips. Don't make a sound.
Listen to yourself. Listen without hearing anything.
What a wonderfully weird thing, huh?

NOW MAKE THIS PART LOUD!
SCREAM IT IN YOUR MIND!
DROWN EVERYTHING OUT.
Now, hear a whisper. A tiny whisper.

Now, read this next line with your best crotchety-
    old-man voice:
"Hello there, sonny. Does your town have a post office?"
Awesome! Who was that? Whose voice was that?
It sure wasn't yours!

How do you do that?
How?!
Must be magic.

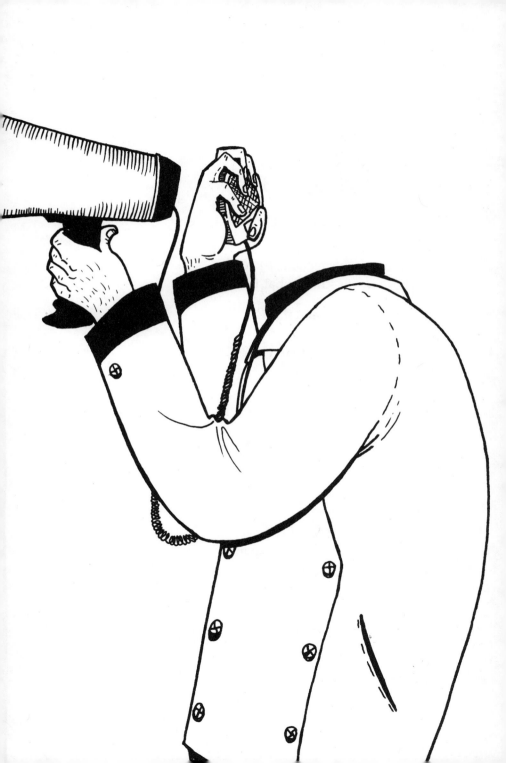

Anteater, Blender, Butthole

Anteater, blender, butthole:
these words know what they're doing.

What does a blender do?
Blend.
What does an anteater do?
Eat ants.
What's a butthole?
A hole in your butt.

Carpet, manslaughter, folklore.
These words suck.

What is a carpet?
No idea.
What is manslaughter?
It's actually slaughtering men or women. Misleading.
What is folklore?
A bunch of folk doing lore? What the fuck is lore?

Absolute nonsense.
We need more words like *toothbrush.*

Two Parties

It's a week before the wedding
    and the bride is with her friends
        (grown women with bright plastic dick jewelry)
    and the groom is with his friends
        ("grown men" or "bright plastic dick jewelry").

I Eat Words

I eat words! Delicious words!
I gobble the words that you make.
Words like *rod* taste like turds,
but *billow* tastes like cake.

I stuff my face with *afterwards*
and wash it down with *hush*.
Dessert must wait till after words
like *hunch* or *flack* or *crush*.

And my dessert won't be *dessert*.
That word is tough to chew.
I'll have a word that's sweet and curt,
like *pony*, *nip*, or *blue*.

On Poets and Farts

Why do poets always talk about the ocean's waves,
about their single file march to shore,
and yet never talk about my grandmother's farts,
which arrive in time, one after the other, with equal
    regularity?

Are these poets too holy to comment on anything
less than nature's flashiest gestures?
Are we going to spend another millennia searching
for meaning in sunsets and waterfalls?

Or will we finally turn our ear to Grammy's rump
and away from all that pretty stuff,
and hear that foul, muted trumpet sing,
marking the end of an era?

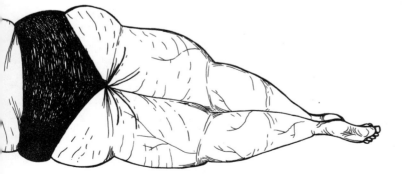

Chameleon

I put a chameleon on a red dildo.

He blushed.

Flowers

On the third of June, at a minute past two,
where once was a person, a flower now grew.

Five daisies arranged on a large outdoor stage
in front of a ten-acre pasture of sage.

In a changing room, a lily poses.
At the DMV, rows of roses.

The world was much crueler an hour ago.
I'm glad someone decided to give flowers a go.

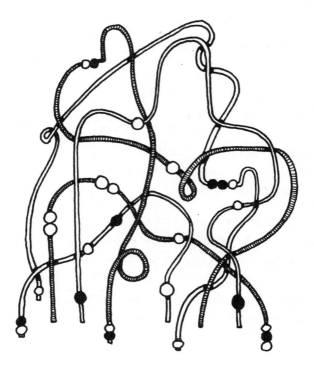

Hell Waits

Hell waits in a doctor's office,
tapping his shoe against a loose strip of carpet,
holding a magazine in front of his face,
trying to look professional,
whilst eyeing the children's toys.

Alfred

You're a bunny, Alfred.
Quit all this "elephant" bullshit.
Look at your little bunny ears.
Look at your adorable whiskers.
Do elephants have little bunny ears?
Do they have adorable whiskers?
No, they don't.

You can't just wake up one day
and decide to be an elephant, Alfred.
The world doesn't work like that.
There are rules, Alfred.
And you want to stomp all over them.
Get over yourself.

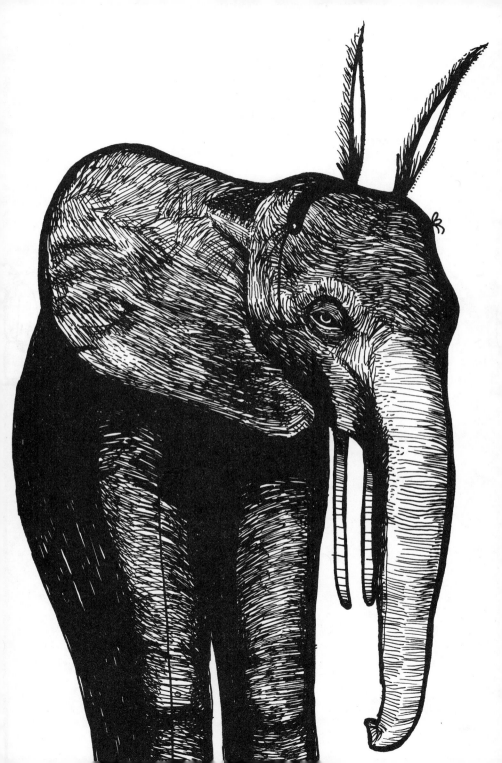

Suits

The influx of suited men on the airport's moving

walkway transformed it into a conveyor belt.

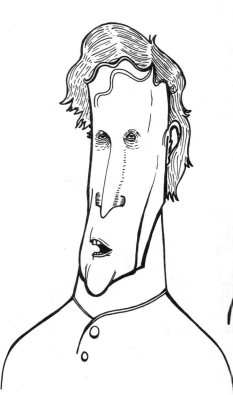

Sully

Sully suffers from a stutter,
simple syllables will clutter,
stalling speeches up on beaches
like a sunken sailboat rudder.

Sully strains to say his phrases,
sickened by the sounds he raises,
strings of thoughts come out in knots,
he solves his sentences like mazes.

At night, he writes his thoughts instead
and sighs as they steadily rush from his head.

Old Sea Captain

Ye Old Sea Captain.

You know, briny breath,
one squinting eye,
chewing a waterlogged pipe,
squatting on a dock post.
A bearded cauldron blabbering bullshit,
crashing through anecdotes
like a radio dial through waves of white noise.

Living legend, he is.
A great American archetype.
So grab your digital cameras
you yuppie fucks.

Fitting

How fitting, she thought to herself
(or just thought, as she was the only person
to whom she had ever thought).

How fitting, she thought, that her words,
after tumbling in her head all day,
came out shrunken
like they were meant for a child.

You

How, may I ask, did you get so *you*,
you beautiful true-to-you doer?
I've met many today but can honestly say
that I've never met anyone you-er.

The Flirt

I could make an easy joke to get you laughing.
Something about a cat and then
the word *pussy* being used ambiguously.

I could tell a sad story to get you crying.
Like how I had a single mother
who started selling handmade yo-yos
to support her only child.

I could tell you an interesting fact to get you nodding,
Like how carpets were first made in the hopes that
      all of the world's grass
would one day be replaced by carpets, or, as they called
      them, "comfy grass."

I could tell you a scary story to get your teeth chattering,
Something about a really old man, sitting in a squeaky
      rocking chair, pointing at you.

What are you in the mood for?

My Rabbit's Foot

I've got a rabbit's foot and I feel lucky that I have it,
but I still know that it must've come from one
   unlucky rabbit.

Onion

You had many layers like an onion.
Wait, no, like an artichoke—with your
layers arranged like snake scales, not
stacked like coats of paint.

Be sure to call in a year or so and
tell me whether I was lifting heavy
stones off your bunker door or
plucking petals off your face.

I Fuck Sluts

Sluts! Sluts! I fuck sluts!
Sluts get fucked when I fuck sluts!
No ifs, ands, and/or buts!
I fuck sluts! I fuck sluts!

Nice girls are nice, but no good for nut-sucking.
They'll need a serene night to green-light a butt-fucking,
but that'll be easy with sleazy ol' slut-fucking!
Boo to the nice girls! Praise be to slut-fucking!

I have a list. A list? Yes, a list of all the sluts I've missed.
I've never fucked or sucked these sluts and thus my nuts
    are fucking pissed.
So when I fuck the lucky slut, my nut removes her
    from the list—
another dumb cumbucket struck from my nut-sucking,
    "suck it, slut!" slut-fucking bucket list.

Sluts can be white, black, brown, pink, or almond.
They can be skinny with big tits or be skinny with
    small ones.
Sluts can be perky, preppy, or posh,
with their brains and their clothes all shrunk
    from the wash.

But other sluts are pretty and funny and smart.
They can lift all your thoughts from your dick
to your heart.
They can talk about science, music, or art.
They can put you together or pull you apart.

But don't trust these sluts! Don't! Don't you dare!
They'll force you to trust them and love them and care.
And then they'll be gone and then you'll be aware
of that hole in your heart that that dumb slut left there.

Incomparable

You're incomparable like a...
Shit.
Like a...

Gangly

I'm a gangly kid,
one of those drunk marionettes,
one of those baby giraffes with inner ear syndrome.
A flailing stork in high winds. A stilted freak.

I am an easel—not symbolically—structurally.
I attempt to dance and become a tornado of elbow.

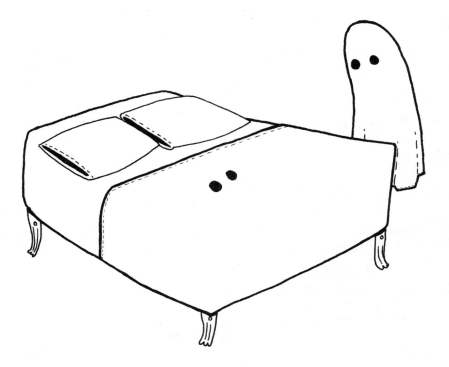

Advice

If the poem you're writing is silly and dumb,
make sure that it rhymes at the end. Bum.

Can I Have a Word?

Can I have a word, please?
It can be any word.
Just give me a word.

We can share all the rest.
Just let me have one.
It can be anything.
I'd take *canteen* or *avid*.
I'd even settle for *timely*.

But you can't use my word,
whatever it is,
without asking.
Because it's my word.

And I'll almost always let you use it when you ask.
Unless, for example, my word is *wonderful*
and you want to use it to describe a movie I haven't seen yet
or a movie I saw already and didn't care for.

I really want *everything*.
That's my first choice.
Flabbergasted is a close second.

Fear

The first was acro-claustro-homo-arachnophobic,
    terrified of being trapped in a very small,
    very high-up place with a bunch of gay spiders.

The second was avio-coulro-glosso-metrophobic,
    terrified of being forced to read poetry
    to the clown public on an airplane.

The third was octo-oneirogmo-kathiso-lutraphobic,
    terrified of having eight consecutive wet dreams
    whilst sitting on a pile of otters.

The fourth was afraid of snakes.
    What a pussy!

Flower Sex

Flower sex! Flower sex!
Flex those sexy flower pecs.
Good old April shower sex
that lasts for half an hour sex.

Yeah! Flower power her!
Devour her! Don't cower, sir!
Put the petal to the medal
and powerfully deflower her!

Angel

The snow lay gently upon the ground.
The poo lay gently upon the snow.
The boy lay gently upon the poo.

And the boy made a snow angel.

An angel
with a white body made from heaven's ashes
and a brown heart made from a dog's
    gastrointestinal tract.

Your Mom

If I had a million dollars, I would pay your mother
   to have sex with me.
Afterward, I would probably invest the remaining
   nine hundred ninety-nine thousand nine
   hundred ninety dollars.
Burrrrrrn.

Toast

I'd like to propose a toast:
sourdough pumpkin bread.
Thoughts?

The Letter

I wrote you a letter,
and then another letter,
and another, and another,
until I wrote you a word.

So I wrote you a word,
and then another word,
and another, and another,
until I wrote you a sentence.

So I wrote you a sentence,
and then another sentence,
and another, and another,
until I wrote you a letter.

I hope it finds you as I found you.

Yours truly,
Yours, truly.

Rock Bottom

I've
hit rock
bottom.

What's
a guy
to do?

I
certainly
can't
head
upward,
so
I'll
try
digging
through!

Us

I'll love you until I'm dead on the outside.
I'll give you every one of my mortal seconds.
I'll never leave your side.
I'll die holding your hand.
But after that, I want some "me time."

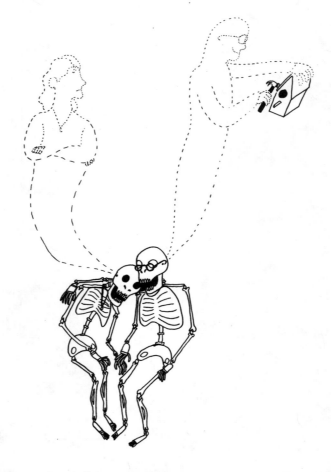

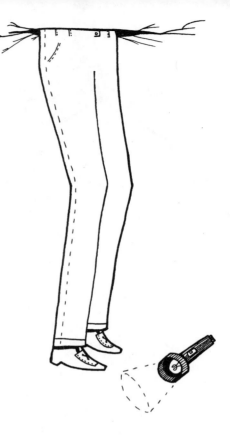

Searching

I'm not looking in every nook and cranny for it.

I'll do the nooks.

No way I left my keys in some fucking cranny.

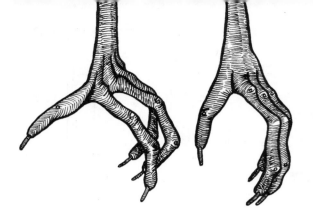

Baby Turtles

Eight baby turtles scurry to shore.

Wait, seven—now six—now five—now four!

Two more gone, two left in the race,

both of them sprinting and hoping to place.

The first gets second, the second gets third,

and first place goes to the now well-fed bird.

Cup of Joe

There's nothing like a cup of joe,
when the morning's grey and grim and slow,
when the streets collide with the world outside,
when litter lies where lilies grow.

Just drink that smoking cup of black
and feel your feelings surging back.
Plus, spill a drop and a coffee shop
will sprout up from a sidewalk crack!

Sandy Claws

Aw, it's plump, old dandy Sandy Claws.
It's fuckin' Daddy Christmas.
How's it hanging, Sandy Claws?
I'm sure Miss Kringle missed us.
I love you, you big dumb sack of shit.
Come over whenever, I got the fireplace lit.
I'm fuckin' with you!

My Daughter

My daughter,
   on her teeter-totter,
      slaughtered the fresh water otter I bought her.

Just like I taught her.

Entrance

When I walk into a room, you'd think I was one of those long, straight Tetris pieces because everyone's just like, "Oh great, you're here! We've been waiting for you to show up."

Nine to Five

Grooming my cuticles
in an un-roomy cubicle.
The phone rings, duty calls.
Better sell those pharmaceuticals.

Boooop

I will have sex with you if you ask politely.
Or ask.
Or if you politely consent to it.
Or consent to it.
I would like to have sex with you.
Call me back.

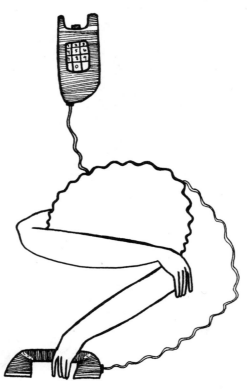

Perched

That guy is sitting on that horse's forehead.

Oh god.

That's not a horse.

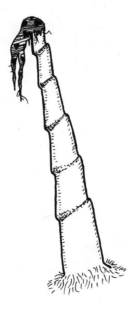

That's a unicorn.

Her

Look at her, balanced on that rotten turtle shell,
conducting the wind with those two moldy corn dogs.
     An old demigod, rightfully covered in bird shit
     in the middle of the park.

     She hasn't lost it. She's found it—
     and it's a disgusting and goofy thing.

     If you don't believe me, have a picnic in the park
     and enjoy gagging on your homemade cooking.

Subtext

hey

                                                        sup?

nothing. u?

                im ona date with u kno who

dude I thawt u and her were thru

                  i did 2 dude I did 2

so how's it goin????

                        badly dude

            she yelled at me for eatin food!

wtf thats fuckingrude

      well shes a bitch I shouldv knewed.

hows the date with such and such?

           she said i used her as a crutch

        she sad i don't talk and i text too much

jesus dude what a butch!

bitch I mean

Pumpkin

Someone carved a face in that pumpkin,
and now it's perched on a stoop, grinning
with the same sinister grin the carver must have had
when he carved it.

And everything I recognize as expressive
(the triangular eyes, that big toothy smile)
is marked by a lack of pumpkin.
A red face of dead space.

And now I'm seeing just the opposite.
I see two spots where the eyes should be,
an open wound where the mouth once sat,
and a fire within, baking the insides.

Martha

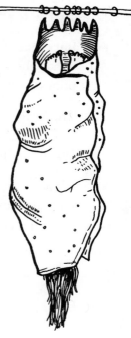

Martha was ugly like a shaven baboon,
   so she wrapped herself up in a
   curtain cocoon.
After a week, she finally emerged
   and she smelled like shit.
   What a psycho!

Disembodied Heads

Severed heads get all the attention.

"Poor ol' disembodied heads,"
cry the townspeople.

But what about the severed bodies?
What about that poor ol' disembodied head's
poor ol' disemheaded body?

The heads roll around moping all day.
The bodies work in the mines.
Without a union!

It's a no-brainer for the no brainers.
Give 'em some respect.
They harvest our coal, for Christ's sake!

Benches

Old men love to sit on benches. They do! All day.
If you see an empty bench, look around.
I guarantee that you will not see any old men.

Old men always sit on benches.
And they always have.

Back in the day,
    baby old men,
        with their baby walking sticks
            and baby dentures,
                would sit on tiny baby benches.

And as they grew,
    from baby old men
        puttering around dragging baby oxygen tanks
            into grown-up old men puttering around
            dragging oxygen tanks,
the benches grew too.

Sometimes,
two old men will sit on a bench together.
And that's fine.
Because it's not a throne.
It's a bench.
And it's for old men.

Count of Six

I'll give you till the count of six.

One.
Now run!
Two.
Go screw!
Three.
Let me be!
Four.
There's the door!
Five.
While I'm still alive!
Six.
Please stay, I love you.

The Commercial

Coupons! Sales! Deals!
Bargains! Free stuff! Steals!
Buy five marked up, get one half price!
Buy two of one thing and get one thing twice!
Earn customer points when you shop at our store!
Redeem customer points to shop here some more!
And we love America! Hip hip hooray!
Every product made right in the US of A.
So come meet our great big American family.*
And be welcomed with a great big American laugh!

*staff

The Nudist

Before I was a nudist, I was a man of many cloths,
but all that changed the day I met a swarm of starving moths.

Homonyms

Homonyms aren't fare.
It's awful. It's tragic.
I say I'm pulling out my hare
and they think I'm talking magic.

There

There goes someone.

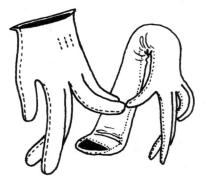

Here goes nothing.

Lou

Lou followed his dreams. Lou followed those things
into studios and boxing rings,
into clown schools and swimming pools,
into plucking little fiddle strings.

Lou followed his dreams. Now he's dirt-poor.
He doesn't have a pillow or bed anymore.
So three cheers for Lou, the follower who
followed his dreams all the way to the floor!

Another Day on the Ant Farm

Another day on the Ant Farm
and still no crops in sight.
The soil's something terrible,
the days are far too bright.
We work the fields, we tend the land,
we check the ground for weeds,
but how are we to farm when
we weren't even given seeds!

There's little hope in sight
and as I sit here all alone,
I wonder if an Ant Farm's
just a place where ants are grown.

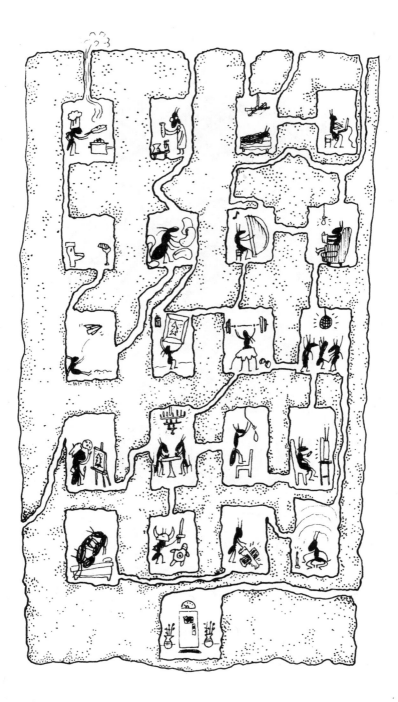

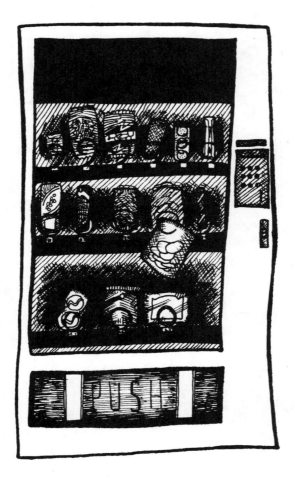

Fuck

Ah, fuck.

The Light

When I die, I hope I don't see a bright light.

Those give me headaches.

After a long life, I don't want to stare into the sun.

I want a calm blackness—
the same shade that coats the back of my eyelids.

Cat Lady

Buried beneath a pile of cats,
in a purring igloo,
is the crazy fucking cat lady.

Who'd have guessed?

Big

When I was little,
I killed ants with a magnifying glass.

And now I'm big.
And I worry I'm doing the same thing with you.

Using You

I worry that
I'm using you,

my love,
my light,
my back-scratcher,
my cooking dickglove,
my sapient baby-maker,
my emotional treadmill,
my long-legged suggestion box,
my immaculate tissue dispenser.

I worry that
I'm using you.

Classic me.

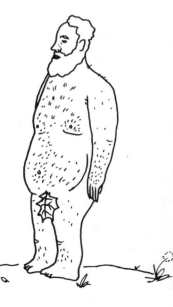

...

I'm a nihilist.
A complete
    and perfect
        nihilist.

Life has no meaning. No point.

Happiness is a chemical coincidence and nothing else
(still "else" though nothing to begin with).

Value is a vast vault of black,
a black that dictates lack.

    Oh, and that accidental rhyme just then meant nothing.

Why are you color-coding things?
WHY?!
What's the point, fascist?

For more, check out my blog.

Armadilla

Armadilla! Armadilla!
On a pilla! On a pilla!
And a giant chinchillo!
And a bigger gorillo!

My Barber Is Bald

My barber is bald, my trainer is fat,
my sponsor is drunken and lazy.
My optometrist is as blind as a bat
and my shrink is batshit crazy.

When you look at who is helping me,
you'll know the reason why
I've remained a bald, fat, drunken, lazy, blind,
    and crazy guy.

Different

Although there's many different brains,
with different stories, different names,
different isn't safe like same,
so same makes most take safer aim.

Who needs those same old, same old fakes?
Today, that same old, lame mold breaks.
I'm me! I'm me! Meet me and see
what a difference difference makes!

Three Little Words

If you were perfect,
I'd tattoo this on my chest.

If you were beautiful,
I'd carve this into a tree trunk.

If you were nice,
I'd write this in a letter.

But you're none of those—

The Martian

One of them Martians came round the house last night.

> Talking in code or some shit.
> Weird fucking things they are.

He rambled for a good ten minutes.

> Didn't listen. Kept staring at his brain
> through that tacky glass head of his.
> I could see his thoughts form. I could see
> them scramble around like ants on hot pavement.
> Dumb and flightless, that's what they are.

He eventually left. Haven't thought of him since.

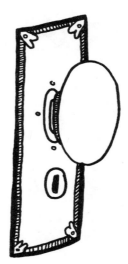

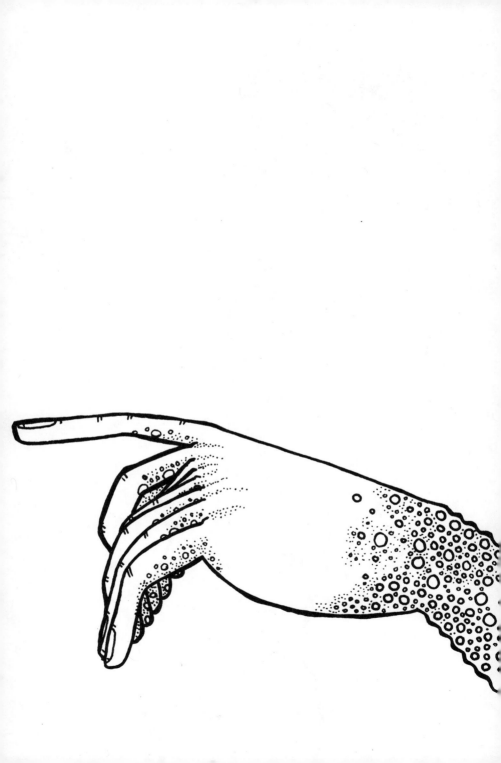

Xia Cobolt

I don't want to die.

It keeps me up at night.

Because I know that when I die, whenever that will be, I'll probably wake up in some futuristic shopping mall, having just spent two space dollars and a mere fifteen space minutes living "my life" by means of one of the future's virtual reality massage chairs. Then I'll get up and watch the long line of people circle through, living "my life" then getting back in line.

And I'll remember who I am again.

I'm Xia Cobolt, a twelve-year-old Pan-Asian Euroamerican girl.

And I'm a fugitive.

Father Time

Father Time is fucking Mother Nature.
He's fucking her good. And he's lasting a long time.
She's loving the shit out of it.
He's doing that thing that makes girls' heads spin.

She's been spinning for years!
I heard that one day, in the future,
he's gonna fuck her right into the sun.
He's done it to chicks before.

Playground

The big bugs buzz and putter about the playground.

They're trying to have fun—to enjoy themselves—
but it's impossible.

Because the playground is made for tiny people,
not big bugs.

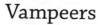

Vampeers

I've seen a vampire transform into a single bat.

I've seen a vampire transform into a number of bats.

I've seen a vampire without any bat-transformation abilities.

WHICH IS IT!?

Split Decision

Since both of us couldn't have you,

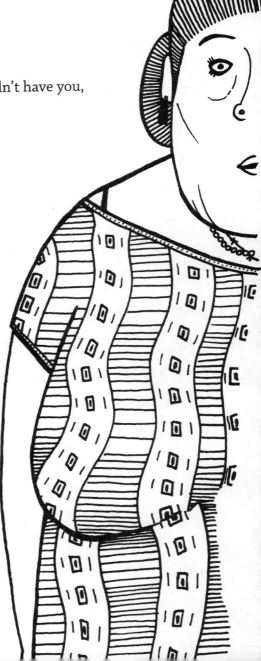

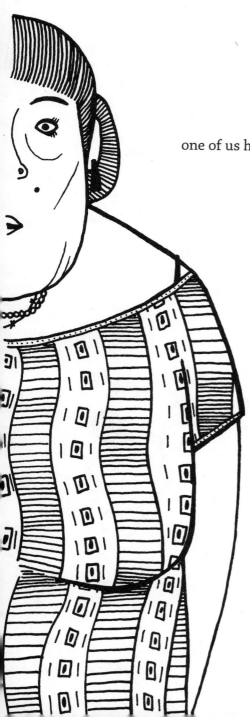

one of us had to halve you.

Bee Guys

Three bee guys were scared for their lives.
They broke out of their hives,
then broke out in hives.

They screamed, "We miss our honeycomb home!"
and three wives from the hive screamed, "Honey, come home!"

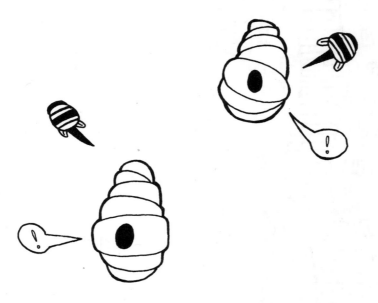

Hold the Cheese

I'll have a cheeseburger.
Hold the cheese.

Hold it in your hand until it melts—
until it bears the shape of that voluptuous palm of yours.

Then put it on my burger.

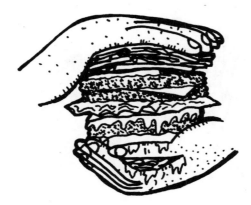

This Hour

I need to make this hour last,

    so attach a beach to the top of my hourglass.

Time Blows

Life is an open book.
　　　　Time is an oscillating fan.

I've had to learn to skim-read because
　　　　before I can read more than a few paragraphs,
that fucking airhead comes circling back,
　　　　blowing pages like a medieval prostitute.

The cool air feels nice, though.
　　　　Sometimes, when my head aches,
I let my eyes relax
　　　　and I enjoy the breeze as the words blur.

My Stamen

We pollinated all night long and when the
　　　　sunlight came, my lover was gone.

Secret Ingredient

You said your secret ingredient
            was a pinch of love.
And that may be true.
            But I taste cinnamon.

            And I hate cinnamon more than I love.

Confession

"No one understands me"

    it slipped out in
    a timid whisper

        as she combed her beard.

Feels

It feels good to love an angel.
It feels better to fuck an angel
with her wings pinned back
like a recently archived butterfly.

The Fall

Mid-October,
with leaves spilled
like colored pencil shavings—

the streets dicing our town
into neat, unfair portions—
and me, eatin' that pussy.

Touch Me Back

"Touch me back,"
      you said, like a pirate talking to a masseuse.
"Right away, Captain,"
      I replied, forgetting that you couldn't hear
      that connection that I made in my head.

Life

Life, man.
Life is a river.
It twists and turns and has fish.
Life is hope. Hope is love.
So transitively, love is a river, too.
Pretty neat, huh?

Imagination

They say adults have no imagination. Not true.
Just instead of dinosaurs and spaceships, they imagine
silence and the new babysitter bent over the coffee table.

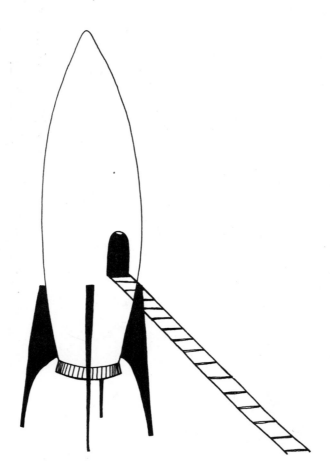

TreeHouseTree

I went out to play on Christmas Day
and thought, "Hey, wait a minute!
My tree has a house in it!
And my house has a tree in it!"

Above and Below

You little perfect thing, you.
At once, I stand in awe and condescend,
my puppy, my goddess.

One and Another

When one meets another,
he or she must treat him or her kindly.
If a third were to enter,
he or she must be swiftly executed to avoid confusion.
Got it?

Senator

Senator, what bright eyes you have!
    The better to light paths with.
Senator, what a sharp tongue you have!
    The better to cut the fat with.
Senator, what broad shoulders you have!
    The better to carry you with.
Wait, why is your chest beeping?
    God bless America!

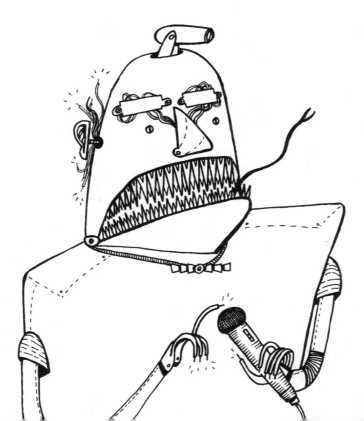

Boston Poem

The Boston people pass the time
by making all their stories rhyme.
Like, "Yesterday, me and my ma
watched the Sox game at the bar."

Sharks

You're afraid of sharks?
Really?
They don't even have bones!
They have cartilage.
Are you afraid of ears too?

Our Father

Our father, who art in heaven,
hallowed be thy name,
hollow be thy promises
and shallow be thy shame.
Thy kingdom come.
Thy will be done
on earth as it is in heaven.
On a scale from one to ten,
our Lord is totally eleven.
Give us this day our daily bread,
toasted close to dawn,
and forgive us our trespasses
as we shoot those who trespass on our lawn,
and lead us not into temptation,
such as pot or porno,
but deliver us from evil
(if not delivery, then DiGiorno).

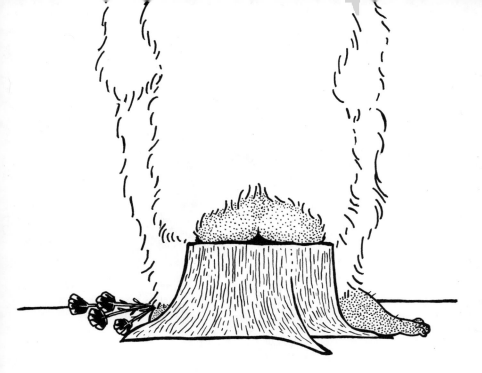

Sasquatch

The Sasquatch squats, flowers in hand,
on an old stump by the riverbed.

She's not coming. He knows that by now,
but he stays put—tracing circles in the dirt
with his big toe.

Overhead, the birds sing their condolences.
A fox passes and offers a bite of dead squirrel.
The monster politely declines.

As the sun tucks itself behind the horizon,
his eyes close, his chin meets his chest,
and the flowers slip from his grasp.

Socrates

Deep in the bowels of Athens,
Socrates is having the squirts—
his body, like the aqueducts,
giving way to a long, watery movement—
hunched head to hands and elbows to knees.
Thinking pretty hard now ain't ya, buddy?
Yeah, I bet you are.

Light Up

She could light up a room with her smile.
And she could really light one up with her flamethrower.

Wind

I wrote down the words that I needed to say but

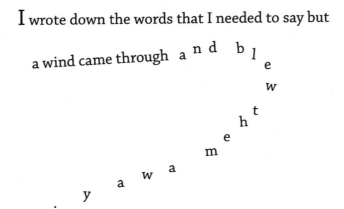

They

"Well, man, you know what they say."
No, I don't. I don't know what they say.
I don't even know who they are.
Who is this *they*?
They seem pretty smug.
They seem to think they know shit.
Fuck them.

Timmy

Timmy took tools and toys and rocks
and played all day in the quicksand box.

Scarf

I wear a scarf
        to keep my words warm.
So you will smile when
        they smack you in the face.

Wise

Babies are the puppies of people.
You feel me?
> I hope you feel me.
> 'Cause I'm feeling like I should be felt right now.

Check this out—
> your first floor's ceiling is your second floor's floor.
> Whoa, right?

Bet you didn't know the plural of *house* is *hice*
or that all dogs are male and all cats are chicks.

> WHO IS THIS GUY?! HOW DOES HE KNOW
> SO MUCH?!?!

(I'm afraid I might die alone.)

Preposition

This is a fine form to make a prepositional
   proposition in.
The proposition is this: prepositions are
   fine to end a sentence with.

Judge Jesus

I said, "You can't judge me.
          Only Jesus can!"

He said, "Well I can 'cause
          I'm a judge and
          'cause you just killed a man."

Fireflies

Hey, fireflies! Fly higher, guys!
Fly high above this place.
Till a sky rise is a wire's size.
Then fly off into space.

I catch stupid bugs in jars
but you're not bugs you're baby stars!

Land of Really Fucked Thoughts

I come from the Land of Really Fucked Thoughts,
where babies are bound by umbilical knots,
where dead horses pile on dandruff-stuffed cots,
where burn-victim monkeys drink blood-and-pus shots.

I come from the Land of That Just Ain't Right,
where young boys like fisting their hamsters at night,
where boxers use AIDS-ridden needles to fight,
where an Alzheimer's orgy's a regular sight.

I don't want to stay but I know I can't leave it.
I needed to tell you but please don't reread it.
I hope this sounds silly and you can't conceive it,
because you're here the second you believe it.

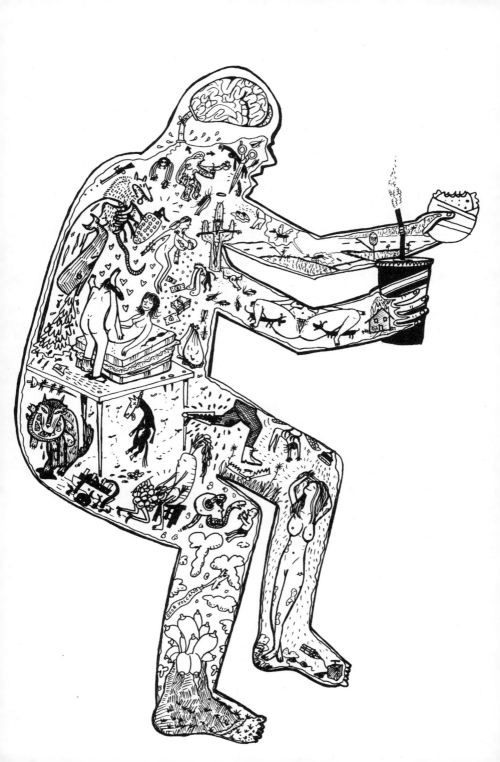

Bombs

The first bomb dropped unheard,
unlike the loudly dropped second and third;
then the final bomb dropped from the sky to the ground
and the last-seen bomb made the last-heard sound.

The Seaward

"You're a cunt,"
I said to the cunt.

"Well, you're a cunt, too!"
replied the cunt to the other cunt,
apparently.

And far away, fresh moss continued
to fill in our initials.

Rollersnakes

duh, duh, duh, duh,
duh, duh, duh, duh,
DUM! DUM!
ROLLERSNAKES!

duh, duh, duh, duh,
duh, duh, duh, duh,
DUM! DUM!
ROLLERSNAKES!

Silly

I love being silly, don't you?
Boing, boing, boing. Poo!
Be silly when you're giddy!
Be silly when you're tired!
If your job is superserious,
be silly till you're fired!

Perfect

I love you just the way you are
but you don't see you like I do.
You shouldn't try so hard to be perfect.
Trust me, perfect should try to be you.

Mmmmmm

I like that thing you do with your tongue.
What do you call it?
Speaking?
Yeah, I dig it.

She Waits

She waits. How beautifully she waits.
How impossibly lovely she is
with a thing so passive.

With what weight she waits,
making her bus or boyfriend
(or whatever she waits for)
seem like a first brunch with Christ.

She waits regally, in perfect contrast
to the drooling buffoon describing her.

Put You in My Pocket

Could I crush you, young lady,
and put you in my pocket?
You would fold beautifully, like
fifty-dollar-bill beautifully, not
origami-swan beautifully.

We could unwind by the
glass lakes of romance or tangle by the
dank wetlands of perversion—
as long as we're together.

All Clear

I pood and wiped,
the wipe was clean,
'twas the closest to happy
I've ever been.

The Biker Gang

The biker gang rode for years and years
through blood and sweat and mud and tears,
through snow and sand and dust and leaves,
and the poor old guys were just looking for sleeves.

Linda

Linda went skydiving
with her pet rat, Max,
and it looks like she
mixed up the parachute packs.

Donald

No matter our race or color or creed
or way of life or species or breed.
No matter our height or girth or scent,
we all hate Donald because Donald is a fucking dick.

Unstick Me

Unstick me, woman. Dial it down.
       Your grip is an aging chicken's and yet,
       here I am—stuck, sticked.

Don't make me whip out a cheap lamp
       and melt this cell into a motel room.

From the Puppy's Perspective

I'm stuck in this thing and I'm wanting to leave.
There are holes in the thing that hiss when I breathe.
And the more that I sit here, the more I believe
that I'm stuck in this thing and won't ever leave.

Back at the kennel, the whole cage was ours
but maybe these walls are better than bars,
or maybe I'm hurtling skyward to Mars
and maybe those holes are actually stars!

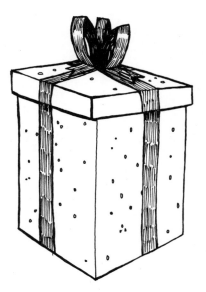

Conversation

"Well...,"
      she said, unwell.
"Well...surely...,"
      she continued, unwell, unsure.
"Listen," he said.
      But nothing.
      Just some rain tapping a window out of boredom.

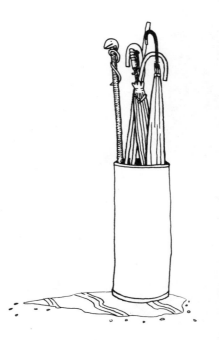

Heart Surgeon

In his long career as a heart surgeon,
in his life full of valves and ventricles,
full of tumors and heartache,
rumors and arteries.
In all those years of blood and tears,
he'd never seen anything like this before.

Routine

The flies do their daily exercise routine,
    buzzing and twisting around the mounds of shit
        in my front lawn.

How happy they must be darting through the stench,
    taking deep breaths of airborne fecal particles
        rather than that stale chemical fertilizer.

The shit is where it's at. The flies know that.
    When the dancing is over, they collapse onto the poo
        and stuff their faces with it.

Hanged

I hung myself today. Hanged? Whatever, point is I hanged myself today and I'm still hanging.

I feel fine. Just bored. I keep hoping that someone will come home and cut me down but then I keep remembering that if I knew someone like that I wouldn't be up here. Bit ironic, right? Or is that not ironic? I read somewhere that, like, anything funny is, in some way, ironic. But I don't know if it's funny or not. I don't think my brain *owns* "funny," you know?

I feel taller. I like that.

I've never been away from my shadow for this long. It had always clung to my feet, parting momentarily for a quick dive into the swimming pool. But never for five hours. I like it. There's three feet of space between my two and the floor.

I wanted something this morning. I may be stuck. But at least I'm three feet closer to it.

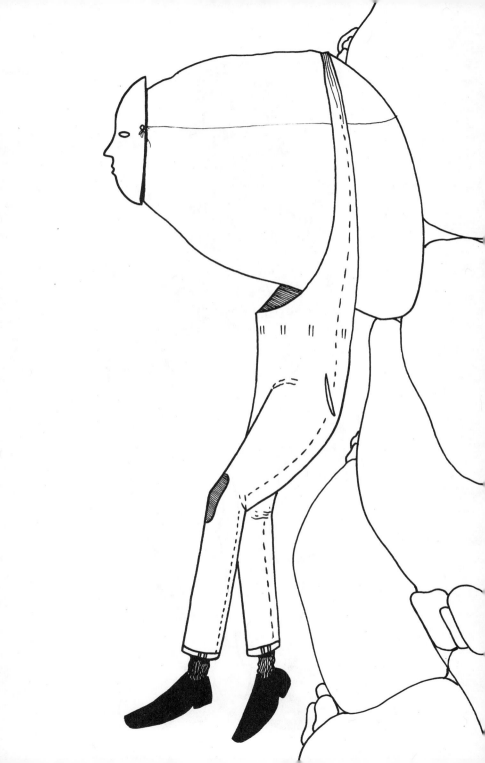

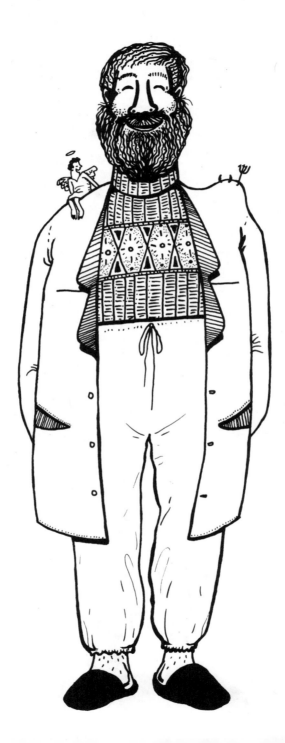

Nothing

Are you terrified, as I am,
of nothing?
Nothing scares me more
than nothing.

"What's going on?" I ask, trembling.
Don't you say it.
Don't you dare.

Stars

The stars buzz around me
all lovely and green,
with a bright swirl of dusty stuff
dancing between.

As I lay down in bed,
I still can't conceive
that they'll carry on gamboling
after I leave.

Hello, My Old Friend

Hello, my old friend!
You silly old clown!
How's that mountain of life
you've been tumbling down?

How's that little line segment with infinite points?
Has the red rust of time been kind to your joints?

How's that worn path of safety?
Has it led you astray?
What's that? How am I?
Oh, I'm okay.

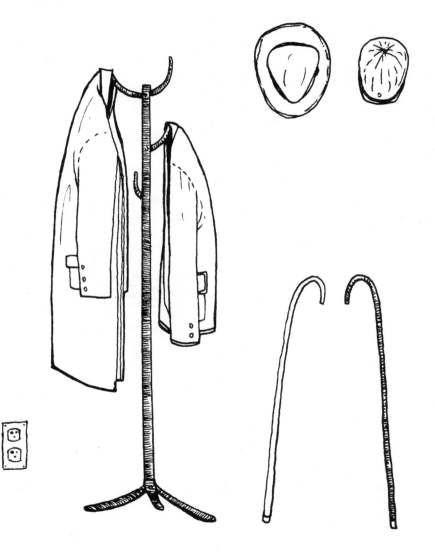

:'(

The heartbroken high schooler
compares his search for love
to his laptop's search for WiFi.

So random, so fickle, so futile.
Cooooooooool.

Gay Parading

Why do these gay guys always parade around,
　　being all gay?

Like, two months ago,
I was at this gay pride parade
and this one guy on a big gay float
kept parading around, real gay-like.

Same thing happened fourteen months ago.
Same spot.
Same guy.
Parading around.

Jesus

I found Jesus once.
He was in a diner eating hash browns.

He had one of those long booths all to himself.
He wasn't being greedy or anything.
Place was pretty empty.

I watched him play the crane game on the way out—
the one with the metal claw and the cuddly mass grave.
He kept going for a rabbit in overalls.
The claw couldn't lift it.

Eventually, he gave up and left.

I tried for a bit.
The rabbit's just too heavy.
I think whoever owns this thing
put an unmovable toy rabbit
in there just to fuck with everybody.

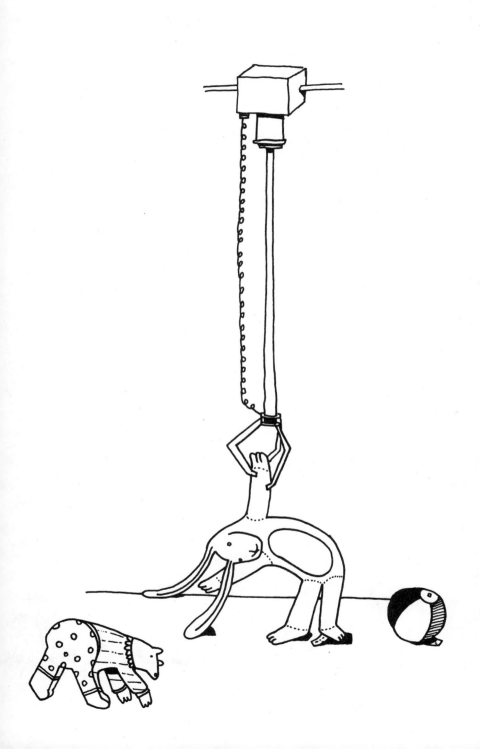

Strange Adjectives

Me,
with my strange choice of adjectives.

You,
with your muscular teeth and clockwise vagina.

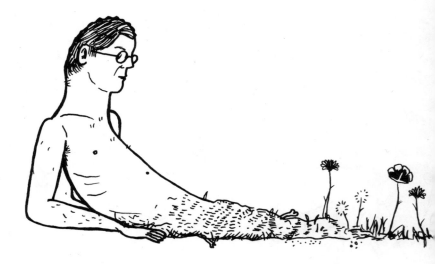

Gone

That small turn she
did, that one swift
pivot, the one she
did by the water with
flats scratching the
sidewalk, her hair
catching up seconds
afterward, fucked me.

Gypsy

On Wednesday morning, clear and calm,
        I went to Astor Place
and had a Gypsy read my palm
        or maybe just my face.

She said my heart was heavy
        and my head was stuffed with lies.
But things like that weren't on my hand,
        they hid behind my eyes.

The room is dull and dank and cold but at
least I have a hand to hold.

Bar Joke

A priest, a rabbi, and a horse walk into a bar.
The bar bursts into flames. The horse escapes,
only to drown in a lake later that night.
As for the priest and the rabbi? Turns out
they were just two other horses. My mistake.

I'm Smart Like a Genius

I'm smart like a genius.
You're dumb like an idiot.

I'm handsome like a prince.
You're ugly like a regular person.

You're slow like a dumb slug.
I'm fast like a cheetah. Nice knowing ya, SLUG!

You're poor like one of those people who shops at
    that stupid puppet store.
I'm rich like the guy who owns that stupid puppet store.

Your girlfriend sucks.
I don't have a girlfriend which is way better 'cause your
    girlfriend sucks!

You're clumsy like a bad waitress.
I'm suave like a good usher.

You're weak like an old plastic spoon.
I'm strong like a really good-looking guy.

I'm two thumbs up. Way up.
You're two thumbs down. Oops!

You're an ant.
I am the wise praying mantis.

When you walk around, people point and laugh.
When I walk around, people point and smile.

You suck.
I don't.
I don't suck.
You do.

I'm smart like a genius.
You're dumb like an idiot.

The Grade

My first draft got a B+,
so I made one small revision.
I got the paper back.
What the fuck's an F÷?

The Farmer

The lying farmer tries to sleep.
He's drifting off while counting sheep.
Tucked in wool, hand-knitted covers,
the farmer counts his former lovers.

I Want to Beat You to Death

I want to beat you to death with a blunt object.

I want to grab one of those high-end fashion mannequins by the ankles and bash your rib cage in.

I want to sharpen fifty pencils, bind them with a rubber band, stick the lead ends in your mouth, and punch the erasers.

I want to strap you to a bed of nails and then strap that bed of nails to the hood of my car so I can watch you suffer as we drive over speed bumps in a mall parking lot during an earthquake.

I want to burn your dog in front of you, mix his ashes with gunpowder, melt his bone-shaped name tag into a small metal ball, load it all into a musket, and shoot you in the face with him.

I want you to somehow survive a terrible car crash and then somehow not survive a small fender bender on the way back from the hospital.

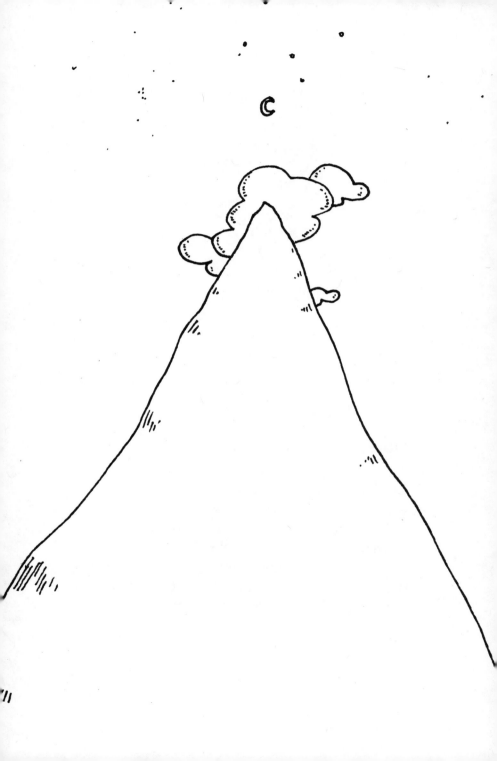

Don't

Don't talk with your mouth full
and don't breathe with your throat full
and don't swim with your stomach full
and don't dance with your colon full
and don't fear with the ground full,
full of your poop, that is, because it will become soil.
What a world.

Public Speaking

The nudist, sweating, with smudged ink filling in the cracks of his palm, approached the microphone, took a deep breath, and imagined the audience clothed.

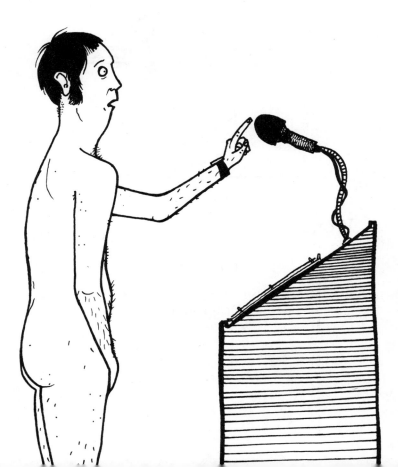

Woman

I. AM. WOMAN.
I am, quite simply, woman.
Deal with it, pigs.

Strange

I feel strange.
Half light-hearted, half heavy-handed.
You know when you get a song stuck in your head
and you can't get it out?
I hate that.
That's sort of what this feels like.

I feel better.
Less panicked, more confused.
But a good confused.
You know that feeling of warm water
running down your back
when washing your hair?
I love that.
That's sort of what this feels like.

I feel great.
And nothing.
This is just what I needed.
A warm bath and a quick nap.

Sirens

I feel poetic when I say that the group of young
teenage girls at the mall

rattled my psyche
    like wailing sirens

and that their freshly developed breasts
    could make for quite tempting cider

should Satan decide
    to pick and press them.

I feel honest when I say that the group of young
teenage girls at the mall

rattled my psyche
    like the other group of teenage girls I once
    saw scissoring in a porno,

and that their freshly developed breasts
    made me wrestle my inner lunatic to
    the ground,

bind his hands behind his back
    and draw him a crude sketch of the young
    girls scissoring to keep him from screaming.

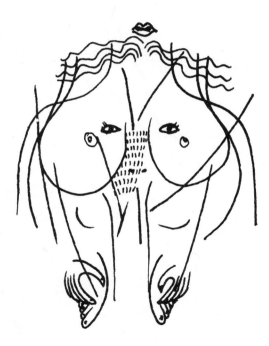

God

Is there a God? I haven't a clue.

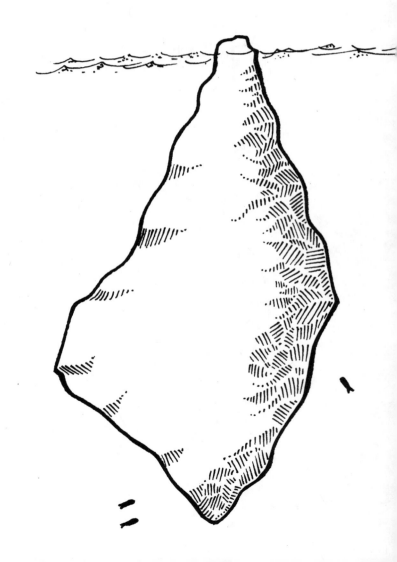

If there is, it's not me, so it's gotta be you!

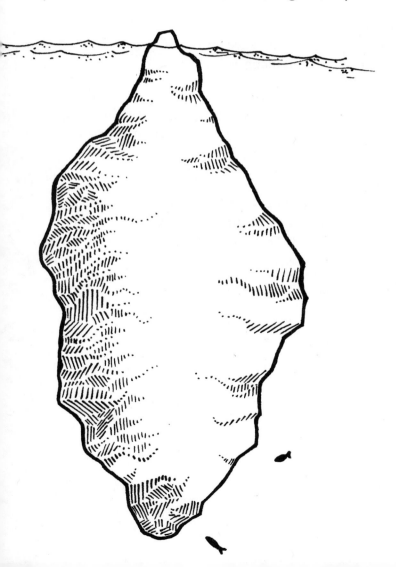

Crazy

You think I'm crazy?
HA! That's real funny.

If I were crazy, would I have written a twelve-hundred-page novel without using a single vowel?
No. 'Cause I did. And I'm not crazy.

If I were crazy, would I be able to predict the future by dropping empty tuna cans into an open drain in my backyard?
No. 'Cause I can. And I'm not crazy.

If I were crazy, would I love to slit your fucking throat just to watch the color drain from your face and onto that cleanly pressed collared shirt of yours?
Yes. I would love that if I were crazy.

But I'm not crazy.

Mannish

People say you look like a man
because of your arm hair.

Don't listen to them.
It's your jawline.

The Epiphany

He was fucking a pussy and sucking a dick,
   his happiness fully depleted,
when he noticed the people attached to those organs,
   and instantly knew what he needed.

No to Drugs

I said no to drugs once.
I looked a bag of weed right in the face
and, like a loving but firm father,
I said, "No."
I was really high.

Ashley

Little Ashley hung magazine spreads on her wall,
after picking the magazines out in the mall.
Models and actresses, singers and more,
with cleavage and makeup and glamour galore!

All of her heroes were finally nearer.
Her whole room looked perfect—except for the mirror.

Clowns

Most people fear

the evil clown,

squeaking his big red nose in a dark barn.

I fear

the off-duty clown,

out of his costume,
impossible to spot,
sitting next to me on a bus.

Turn-Ons

The way her hair barely touched her shoulders,
        like it knew to stop growing there.
The way her lips teased each other when she spoke,
        parting and embracing with every syllable.
The way her tight virgin nostrils twitched and spasmed
    in the moonlight,
        quivering like two horny monks.
The way her curly, almost pubic eyebrows framed her
    fishy, moistened eyes.

    I'm a face guy.

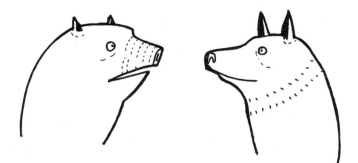

Pigs Are Smarter Than Dogs

Pigs are smarter than dogs.
That's a fact.
That is "science," if you will.
Will you?

Pigs are smarter than dogs.
I love my dog.
I also love eating bacon.

So I can stop eating bacon
or I can continue playing a quiet
and aggressive role in the genocide
of a species whose intelligence sits
safely in the middle of my "worthy of real love" spectrum.

Or I can continue eating bacon
and admit that my love for my dog is a sham,
a hollow and meaningless relationship born
of my own insecurities and years of confirmation bias.

He likes me because I feed him.
That's it. Fuck him.
Bacon is delicious.

A Ghost Story

Two young boys in corduroys
      were playing with a ball.
Two young boys heard one strange noise,
      coming from the hall.

The boys stood still, well, still until
      the door swung open wide.
And a ghostly chill and a real ghost, Bill,
      were heaved the heck inside.

The brave boy stood, as the brave boy would,
      and said, "Hey, listen Bill!
We're here to hear you, not to fear you.
      Tell us what you will."

The other boy wheezed and sneezed then seized
      and vomited on the floor.
He shook his brain. He felt insane.
      Nothing was real anymore.

"Ghosts are real?! They're fucking real?!?!?"
      he cried and shook and feared.
For nature's laws were gone because
      a ghost had just appeared.

And on that night of fear and fright,
      the brave boy had his thrills.
And the other one was fucking done
      and swallowed fifty pills.

Look

A fish
in a bag
in a tree
in a bag.

Let's See What the Robots Think

Before we go folding our clothes in a stack,
let's see what the robots think.
Before we go patting ourselves on the back,
let's see what the robots think.

Before we start working or dancing again,
before we start writing love letters to send,
before we start fighting or finding a friend,
let's see what the robots think.

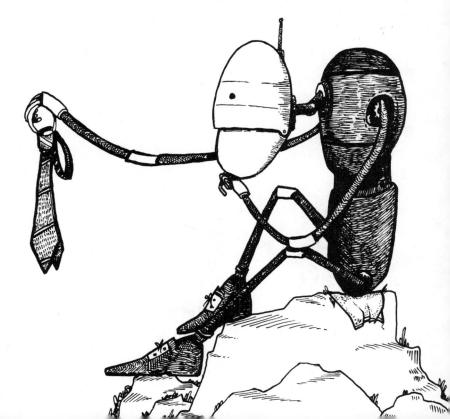

Plate Spinner

I want to be a plate spinner,
I practice all day long.
But I just can't seem to get it right.
What am I doing wrong?

Drink Umbrellas

Those little drink umbrellas that spring up
in the tropics
were invented by a lonely group
of crying alcoholics.

Ed

Ed had a date with a girl that he liked
but she called and she canceled the lunch.
At the biweekly orgy later that night,
Ed pleasured himself by the punch.

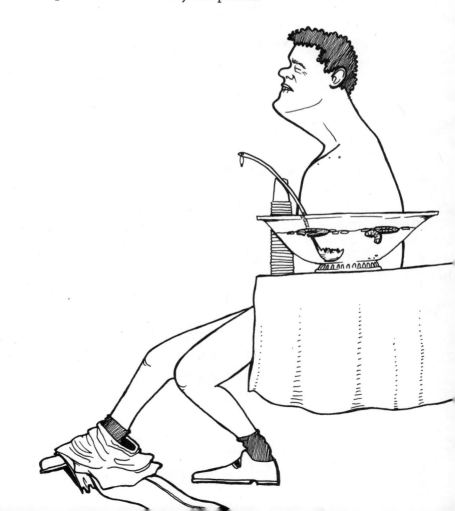

Right, Left

Right when you left, you left me

> cold
> and broken
> and numb—

partly because

> your love warmed me
> and made me feel whole
> and made me feel things I hadn't before—

and partly because

> you left me chopped up in a freezer.

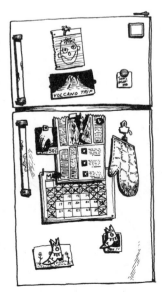

Masturbitosis

I'm the sexiest eukaryote alive.
My mitochondria are so big and powerful.
Look at my fucking Golgi apparatus.
I fucking love it. Yeah, that's it, Golgi.
Keep pinching off lysosomes for me.
I got such a sexy shade of cytoplasm
and my fucking vacuoles mmmmmmm!
Don't get me started,
oh my fuckkkinnggggmmmmmmmm.
Fuck, I can feel it in my nucleus.
It feels so fucking good.
Oh my god. I'm gonna make myself...
I'm gonna...
Fucking Golgi!
Fuck!
I'm gonna.......
I'mmm gonnnnnnnnaaaa

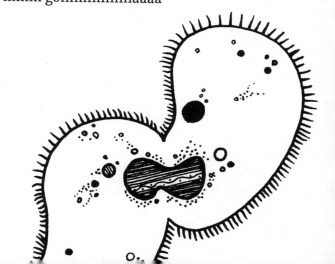

Beautiful

You're the most beautiful girl I've ever seen.
And I know that.

But I can't rediscover it every fucking day.
I can't return to that epiphany
every time my alarm clock goes off.
It's unnatural.

But what I can do, and do quite naturally,
is become jaded and unimpressed by it.
I can see your beauty as normal,
as one of my life's many constants.

I can climb atop its shoulders and travel about,
rolling my eyes at sunsets and rainbows,
dismissing all the beauty of the world as
less than average.

And I can complain to you about it.
And you can deduce your beauty from that.

Relax

Let your hands relax by your sides.
Let your chin rest gently on your chest.
Let each new breath fill you with calm.
Let your mind wander away to a faraway place.
Let me piss on your expensive shoes.
Let me empty your pockets of any valuables.
Let me escape this parking garage as you drift past
     some meadows or some shit.

Him

Ah, there he is.
That motherfucker.
What a tool.

Be Patient

Be patient, be patient.
Rome wasn't built in a day.
It wasn't built at all, in fact.
Rome self-assembled in reaction
to the people's unwavering patience.
So be patient, be patient.

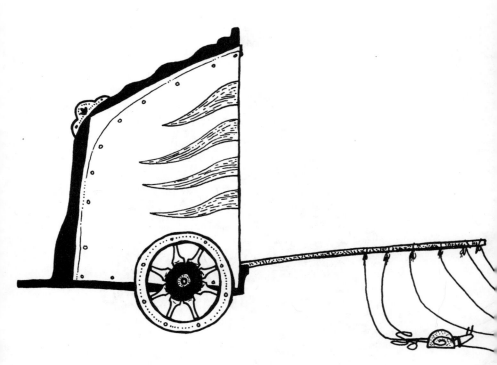

A Final Wish

Cremate me, please
and sprinkle my ashes,

pinch by pinch
on strippers' eyelashes.

The Party

Only after that drunken late-night congress
    had dispersed
and the music had stopped and the walls had caught
    their breath
and the smug fog of dialogue had condensed on the
    empty glasses,
only then did I notice how unhappy you were.

The strobe light had given me stale, unusable snapshots.
Even if I had seen some struggle on you, somewhere,
I would have mistook it for simple social rigmarole
as everyone's behavior reeked of performance.

And only after that night had given into the next day,
and I had stood where you had danced so cautiously,
and I had imagined you sitting in that chair that still
    bared my imprint,
only then did I realize why you felt that way.

Change

I don't expect
to change your mind
with one conversation,

only to chip away at it,
like a woodpecker on a redwood tree.

Rock

Rock on,
>indie rocker!

Rock
>those bongos!

Rock
>that weird African instrument that you
>purchased on that private school field trip.

Rock on
>about that girl who left you because she got
>tired of struggling to get your skinny jeans off.

Rock on
>about the poetry of the universe, armed
>with the knowledge you gained by skimming
>a Wikipedia article on quantum mechanics.

Rock on
>about pain and addiction (itchy beards and
>clove cigarettes, respectively).

Rock
>against the labels.

Rock
>against the system.

Rock
>against the world.

Rock
>against rocking.

Rock.

A Wonderful Day to Be Dead

What a perfect day to be gone and forgotten.
       What a wonderful day to be dead.
Six feet above me, the world's gone rotten
       while I'm rottin' in a coffin instead.

You'll die one day and that day could be
       any one of the thousands ahead,
but I can guarantee that that day will be
       a wonderful day to be dead.

Up Above

From my window seat, the world looks so tiny, the cities so adorably ordered.

Makes me realize just how insignificant people are and just how godlike I am.

Roller Coaster

Our love was a roller coaster.
It had ups and downs and I sat real close to her.
It had a real slow climb and a real quick drop.
I screamed "faster" and she begged it to stop.
I put up my hands and she held on tight.
Not a second of boredom on our rickety flight.
And when it came to a stop at that first safer place,
I said, "Let's do it again," and she puked in my face.

The Pussy

The pussy has become overwhelming.
It's tumbling out of every suitcase,
whirring beneath every floorboard.

Who thought the pussy could become so cumbersome?
It stacks against my front door like fresh snow,
presses its lips against the glass of my kitchen window
like an inmate's wife would do with her regular face lips.

Where the world was once empty, it is now pussy—
as if I'm trying to measure the atmosphere's volume
by means of pussy displacement.

Offence

They let gays marry
and I took offense to that;
then my brother got gay-married
and I took a fence to that.

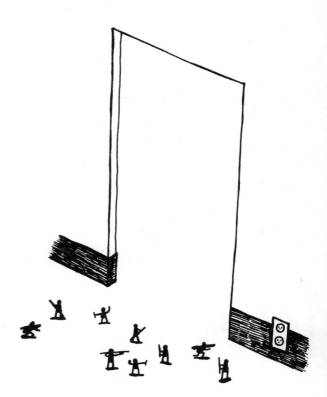

Wooden Soldiers

I bought a box of wooden soldiers.
I bought them from the store.
And now a hundred tiny soldiers
guard my bedroom floor.

So if you're a scary monster-thing
who wants to go to war,
my bedroom door is open.
I'm not frightened anymore.

Walk with Me

Walk with me now if you would
or wouldn't mind
or would mind not walking someone
as I would.

Speak to me now if you must
or mustn't be quiet
or must've forgotten something important
as I must've.

Stay with me now if you can
or can't decide
or can't not stay with someone,
anybody,
as I can't.

Fixed

I gouged my eyes out

only to find another much better
pair behind them.

Listen

You're nothing, Special.

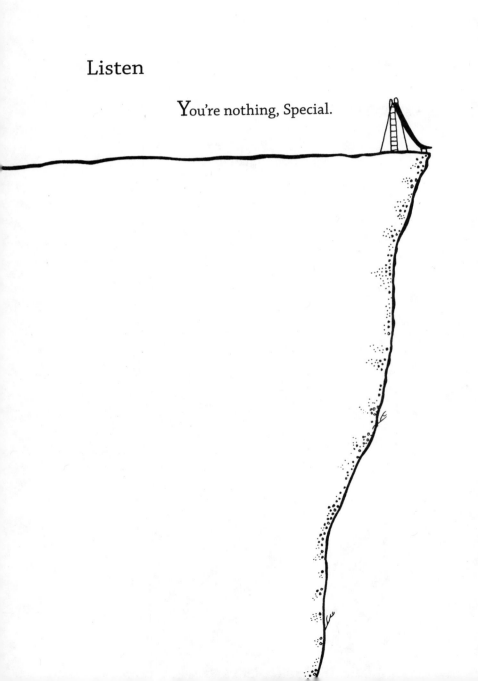

On the Virg

I saw the Virgin Mary in my toast this morning.

She was delicious.

I Don't Give a Fuck

I. Don't. Give. A. FUCK.
Never have, brah. Never will, dude.
You upset? Good! 'Cause I don't give a fuck!

I dress like I don't give a fuck.
I read in a magazine that women find that attractive.
It's probably true, but I don't give a fuck.

People ask me,
"Whoa man, cool outfit, is it hard not giving a fuck?"
Yes. It's very hard. But it's like, fuck it, you know?
I won't start giving a fuck just because it's hard to not
    give a fuck. You may give a fuck but don't you go
    trying to make me start giving a fuck.
Or do.
'Cause I don't give a FUCK!

When I die, I won't give a fuck.
People will remember me for that.
They'll probably write books about me and build
monuments in my name. But I won't give a fuck.
I'll be dead.
But even if I was alive, I still wouldn't give a fuck.
I'd walk past the giant library built in my honor and
just roll my eyes.
An attractive woman would see all this happen and
she would turn to her friend and say—

"See that guy? He doesn't give a fuck. See that
library? It's named after that guy who doesn't
give a fuck. Ooooh, he's kinda sexy."

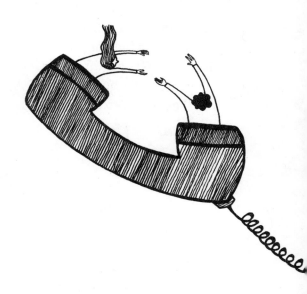

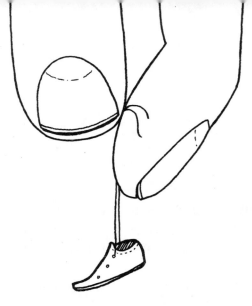

Youth vs. Man

Hey, look! It's the Youth.
The Youth is fighting the Man.
How cute. Get him, Youth! Get him!
Yikes, that was quick.
You'll get him next time!

Fishing

It's unfortunate that the word for "catching fish by piercing their lips with hooks and dragging them onto a boat" is called *fishing*.

To the fish, *fishing* means something different. To fish is to live, to love, to be.

When the more aggressive fish find a lonely swimming human and rip the flesh from its stupid bones—that's called *peopling*.

The Future

I reckon (don't discredit me due to the elderly start)
that in the future, in the far future, if all goes well,
two gay fathers will disown their son
because their son wants to marry his clone.

"It's unnatural!" they'll scream.
"It's an abomination!" they'll cry.

The son and his clone will run away together,
beside themselves, armed only with love.
They will hide in scrapyards and motel rooms
until the bigotry passes, as it always does.

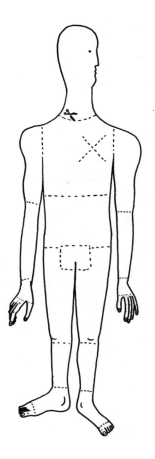

Whole

He poked his penis all over her skin,
pensively feeling for an easy way in.
This man, with his fractal and fragmented soul,
finally felt hole and finally felt whole.

I Can't Stand Trees

I can't stand trees.

They're a bit too theatrical.
They act all dramatic, no static, all radical.
All "Hey, look at me!" All "Hey, I'm a tree!"
All "Hey, stump boy, do you like what you see?"

And I reply, "No! You limp-limbed lug!
You winter leaflet littering bug.
With towering branches and cowering roots,
devouring sunshine and showering fruits.

It's a war they want? Then a war I'll wage.
I'm writing this on paper just to waste...

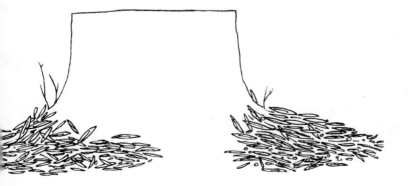

...a fucking page.

Old

I'm old and cold and out of time,
thirteen years far past my prime.
Weary legs from life's steep climb,
I can barely walk let alone think of a fourth word.

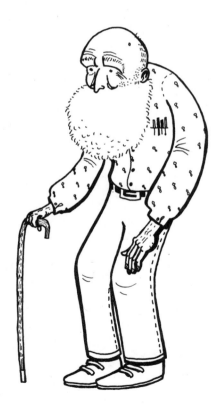

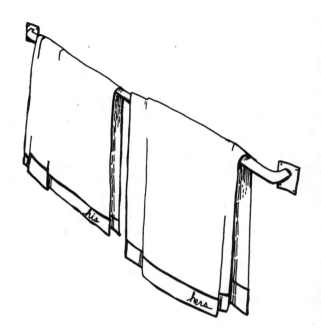

Dating

I'm a gargoyle.
Stuck.
Outdated.
And pretty fucking weird looking.

You're an angel.
Free.
Immortal.
And pretty fucking weird looking, too.

Cyclops

The women ran screaming when the Cyclops blinked.
If only they'd known he'd actually winked.

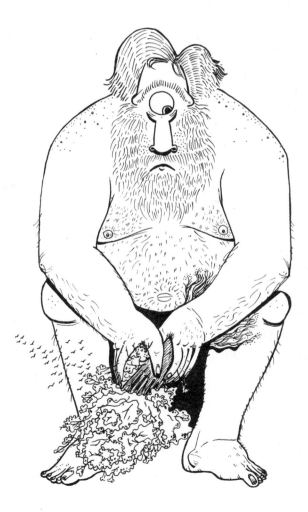

Sea Monkeys

Look at those sea monkeys
puttering around their bowl.

Yesterday, they were a sugar packet
and now they're sea monkeys.

What a dumb miracle.
Dust into animated dandruff.

I've never found the incomprehensible quite this boring.

All that talk about life
and I got a cheap magic trick.

Knots in the Grass

I spend most of my day outside,
crouched to the earth, tying knots in the grass.

I spend most of my year traveling,
looking for fields or front yards, tying knots in the grass.

If you find a knot, you find me,
as I am the only thing tying knots in the grass.

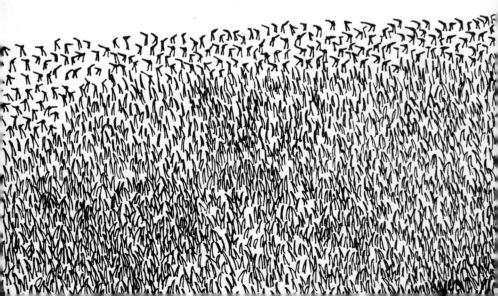

Her Eyes

Her eyes were like fire.
They weren't red or anything.
Not particularly warm, either.
They didn't glow or "appear to glow,"
whatever that means.

But they had that same strange blend of
familiar and miraculous—
and they were always nice to look at
after a long day of doing things.

Hobgoblin

Did you see what the neighborhood hobgoblin did?
On Halloween night, he dressed as a kid!

Fuck in the Woods

Let's fuck in the woods, sweetheart.

Wood to wood, ass to grass,
hands clasped, limbs grasped,
humping parts while nature sways,
licking butts where reindeer graze.

Let's toil, uncoiled, in the soil, soiled.
Broiled in baby oil (tree sap's foil).

Let's flirt with the earth,
with rubber to avert birth
and darkness to assert girth,
no shirt or skirt, just squirting in dirt.

Let's fuck in the woods.

Like

You're like milk,
    tasty and versatile.
You're like a dog,
    loyal and often mistaken.
You're like New York,
    large and in America.
You're like my girlfriend,
    female and actually my girlfriend.

Progress

I almost forgot about you today. A sizable spill of coffee shot me to my feet, holding up my mocha-soaked notebook like an unclaimed child. A dozen eyes found me at once—a security measure meant to bring shame to a klutz breaking his social contract. Attention for shit living. When the pain receded I stood in place and imagined you brushing your teeth.

Bustle

Writers like to talk about how things are or were "bustling."

The market was bustling on a bustling street corner.
In a bustling bakery, the muffins bustled in the oven.
"Don't worry, Rupert, the bus'll be bustling by in five minutes!"

I mean, I get it.
Bustle is a good word.
It makes total sense.

Whenever I'm in a group of more than three people,
all I can hear in my head is
bustle, bustle, bustle, bustle.

I say it to myself, silently,
even when people appear
to be trying to start a
conversation with me.

A cute girl may be right in front of me,
looking at my face and mouthing sounds,
but all I can think of is
bustle, bustle, bustle, bustle.

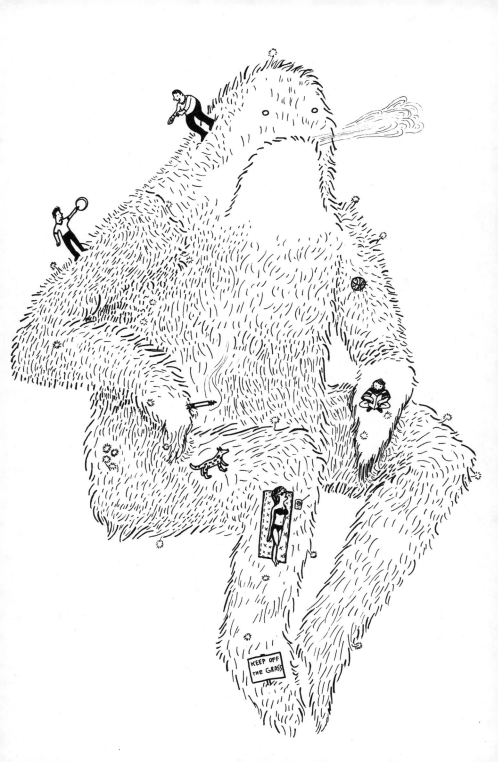

You There

Hey, you there.

Me?

Yeah, you.

Yeah, me?

Yeah, you there.

Me there?

No, you there.

Oh, me here?

Yeah, you there.

So, me?

Yeah. Hey, you there.

Hey what?

Hey.

Hey.

You well?

Yeah, you?

Me?

Yeah, you.

Me what?

Well.

Me well?

No, are you?

Am I?

Yeah.

Am I what?

Well.

Am I well?

Yeah, you well?

Wait, do I well?

No, are you well?

Oh, am I well?

Yeah.

No.

Forever and an Instant

Forever and an instant met up one day,
had a short but lovely talk,
then each went on its way.

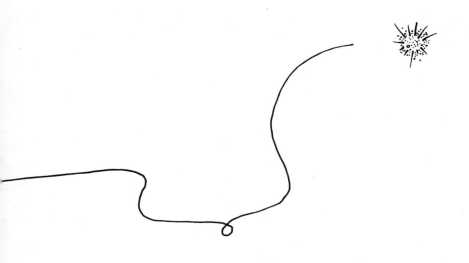

Third Person

He's talking in the third person again.

Look at him,
talking to himself,
about himself,
as if he's talking to someone else
about someone else.

He's about to speak.

"Hey! You!"

Wait, he can't do that.
He can't address "him" as "you."
He *is* "him."

"HEY! YOU!"

Wait a second...
yes?

Acknowledgments

Thank you Richard, Ben, Pippa, and everyone at Grand Central Publishing. I am so grateful.

Thank you to the teachers who inspired me— Mrs. Burridge, Mr. Furlong, and many others.

And to George Carlin and Shel Silverstein.

And Chance. Thank you.

—Bo Burnham

Thank you to my family, Penelope, Abbie, Allan, Lori, Ross, Wendy, Phil, Mickie, and Jennifer; the Theatre School; Ha Ha Tonka; Mrs. Aid, Mr. Smith, and Mrs. Reinholdt, who encouraged me to draw on my homework.

And thank you to Bo. He sure is nice for being so tall.

Big love to you all.

—Chance Bone

Stuck

I'm stuck on this page and I want to break out.
So put me in your brain and walk about!